I PROTEST
A History of Peaceful Protest

VOICES FOR
EQUALITY

Tamra B. Orr

PURPLE TOAD
PUBLISHING

Printing   1   2   3   4   5   6   7   8   9

Voices for Civil Rights
by Wayne L. Wilson

Voices for the Environment
by Tamra B. Orr

Voices for Equality
by Tamra B. Orr

Voices for Freedom
by Michael DeMocker

Voices for Peace
by Wayne L. Wilson

ABOUT THE AUTHOR
Tamra B. Orr is a full-time author living in the Pacific Northwest. She has written more than 500 educational books for readers of all ages. She is a graduate of Ball State University and commonly gives presentations to schools and at conferences. Living in Oregon has helped her participate in different types of protests and rallies, and to recognize the importance of using her voice for everyone's equality.

Publisher's Cataloging-in-Publication Data
Orr, Tamra B.
   Voices for equality / written by Tamra B. Orr.
      p. cm.
Includes bibliographic references, glossary, and index.
ISBN 9781624693755
1. Passive resistance—History--Juvenile literature. 2. Civil disobedience—Juvenile literature. 3. Social action—Juvenile literature. 4. Equality—United States—Juvenile literature. 5. Women—Suffrage—United States—History—Juvenile literature. 6. Income distribution—United States—Juvenile literature. 7. United States--Emigration and immigration—Juvenile literature. 8. Gay rights--United States--Juvenile literature. I. Series: I protest.
 KF4749 2017
 323.41

Library of Congress Control Number: 2017940576

ebook ISBN: 9781624693762

CONTENTS

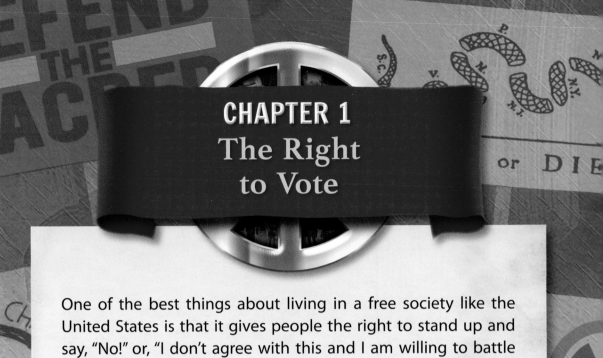

CHAPTER 1
The Right to Vote

One of the best things about living in a free society like the United States is that it gives people the right to stand up and say, "No!" or, "I don't agree with this and I am willing to battle it." That right has been put to the test many times too, because, throughout history, people have been treated badly by other people. Countless tribes and groups have been ignored, abused, and kicked out of their homelands as one culture has conquered another. People have been judged as less worthy because of the color of their skin, the country in which they were born, the religion they follow, or the gender with which they identify. It is not surprising that Elizabeth Cady Stanton, who rallied for women's right to vote, once said, "The history of the past is but one long struggle upward to equality."[1]

These injustices have sparked protests. Groups of people all over the planet, at one time or another, have gathered to say, "No! This treatment is wrong. It is unfair. It should not and cannot be tolerated." They share their messages on signs and in songs, with marches and rallies, and with posts and tweets. Throughout history, protesters have changed the world.

It took many women, many signs, many protests, and many years before women were given the right to vote.

Susan B. Anthony and Elizabeth Cady Stanton

People like Stanton and Susan B. Anthony began working to help women get the right to vote more than 150 years ago. Lucy Burns and Alice Paul, the women who led the National Woman Suffrage Association, carried this fight into the twentieth century. They worked hard to spread their message. They presented petitions to Congress. They gathered to protest on the steps of the U.S. Capitol.

In 1908, the first suffrage parade was held. Twenty-three women walked down Broadway in New York City. Others organized parades in their cities. In May 1910, one parade had 400 women. In 1911, another parade had 3,000 marchers. A year later, parades had more than 20,000 participants. Suffragettes carried banners and wore hats, pins, and buttons with messages on them. In 1913, the day before President Woodrow Wilson's inauguration, thousands of women marched for the right to vote.

Two years later, on October 23, as many as 60,000 women gathered again on New York City's Fifth Avenue. Some came by horse and carriage. Others walked, some with children in hand. Their signs read, "A Vote for Suffrage Is a Vote for Justice," and "You Trust Us with the Children; Trust Us with the Vote." More than 100,000 people watched the parade.

The parade did not convince enough people to change the law, but it made a huge impact. A Kansas City journalist wrote, "It was absolutely overwhelming. Forty thousand women do not spend days getting ready for a five-mile march through crowded streets, and hours marching in a raw afternoon, for a transitory whim. It was the most democratic exhibition I have ever seen in New York."[2]

By January 10, 1917, the women were getting impatient. They decided to try something new. A dozen women went directly to the White House,

Known as the "Silent Sentinels," women protested outside the White House for more than two years. They did not yell at passersby, but shared their message silently.

carrying purple, white, and gold flags and two banners. One read, "Mr. President, what will you do for woman suffrage?" The other asked, "How long must women wait for liberty?" The women picketed the White House that day and the next—and the next. A group was there every day for months. Thousands of volunteers traveled from 30 states to take a turn. Pickets were also held in parks and in front of the U.S. Capitol and Senate office buildings.[3]

Some of the protesters were arrested. They spent time in extremely unpleasant jail cells. During the summer, a number of protesters were attacked while picketing. Police officers and soldiers injured a few of them. Suffragette Inez Haynes Irwin wrote about her experience. She described the "slow growth of the crowds; the circle of little boys who gathered about . . . first, spitting at them, calling them names, making personal comments; then the gathering of gangs of young hoodlums who encourage the boys to further insults; then more and more crowds; more and more insults. . . .

In 1917, the streets of New York City were filled with women carrying placards covered in more than a million signatures of people who wanted women to have the right to vote.

Sometimes the crowd would edge nearer and nearer, until there was but a foot of smothering, terror-fraught space between them and the pickets."[4]

After two years of picketing, suffragettes began burning copies of President Wilson's speeches outside the White House. Suffragettes kept the fires going to urge the president to help women get the right to vote.

Finally, in June 1919, the 19th Amendment was passed. At long last, women were considered equal. They earned the right to vote in the following election.

Across the World

Women in other countries have also fought for the right to vote. In Iran, women finally earned the right in 1963. Other countries took even longer.

South Africa allowed women to vote in 1994, Kuwait in 2005, and the United Arab Emirates in 2006. It took until 2015 for Saudi Arabia to allow women to vote. Tired of waiting, women there decided to protest a new way. On June 17, 2011, dozens of protesters climbed into the driver's seat of their cars. In Saudi Arabia, women were not allowed to drive. According to civil law, they could, but religious laws rule the country as well. The religious laws stated women could not drive—or open bank accounts, get passports, or go to school—unless escorted by a male.[5]

On this June day, women got behind the wheel, but they followed a few rules. They wore full Islamic dress. They had a Saudi flag and a photograph of the king on their cars. Most had a man in the car with them. This allowed them to protest but not be completely defiant. A female blogger from Saudi Arabia, Eman Al Nafjan, told CNN, "We have a saying. 'The rain starts with a single drop.' This is a symbolic thing."[6]

A Half Century Later
Fifty years after the 19th Amendment was adopted, on August 26, 1970, women gathered once more to protest gender inequality. Just as before, 50,000 women marched down Fifth Avenue in New York City. This time, Betty Friedan, head of the National

By getting behind the wheel of a car, many Islamic women showed that equal rights were important—and change was necessary.

The women's march in New York City drew thousands of protesters, far more than even organizer Friedan (third from left) had anticipated.

Organization for Women, led the Strike for Equality March. To show the country how undervalued women were, Friedan suggested all women stop doing any cooking or cleaning. Signs in the crowd read, "Don't Iron While the Strike Is Hot" and "Don't Cook Dinner—Starve a Rat Today."

The women had several goals, including equal opportunity in jobs and education. In addition to the march, some cities, such as Indianapolis, Boston, and Los Angeles, held other events. Women walked into all-male bars and restaurants, carried banners in picket lines, and held sit-ins and teach-ins. The protests sparked several legal changes, and taught many people about the lack of gender equality. "The huge number of marchers, young and old, made a convincing case that this was a movement for everyone," said historian Joyce Antler.[7]

PROTEST SONGS

"Yes, and how many years can a mountain exist
Before it's washed to the sea?
Yes, and how many years can some people exist
Before they're allowed to be free?
Yes, and how many times can a man turn his head
And pretend that he just doesn't see?
The answer, my friend, is blowin' in the wind
The answer is blowin' in the wind."[8]

—Bob Dylan

Woody Guthrie

Protest songs have been around for decades. They use lyrics to state opinions and describe important issues. Musicians have written about injustice, anger, frustration, and protest.

In 1949, Woody Guthrie's "This Land Is Your Land" spoke out about the beauty of the country. It then compared that beauty to the brutality of living in poverty. Singer Bob Dylan wrote several protest songs, including "Only a Pawn in Their Game" about racism; the Vietnam War protest song, "Masters of War"; and the classics "Blowin' in the Wind" and "The Times They Are a-Changin'."

Musicians continue to use lyrics to highlight political issues. In 1992, Garth Brooks' single "We Shall be Free" from his album The Chase created a great deal of controversy. The lyrics spoke about such issues as gay rights and freedom of speech. Some radio stations banned the song entirely. Public Enemy's "Fight the Power" and Bruce Springsteen's "American Skin" are about racism. The Gossip's "Standing in the Way of Control" is about same-sex marriage laws; Radiohead's "Idioteque" is about global warming; and "Civil War" by Guns N' Roses protests war and its profits.[9]

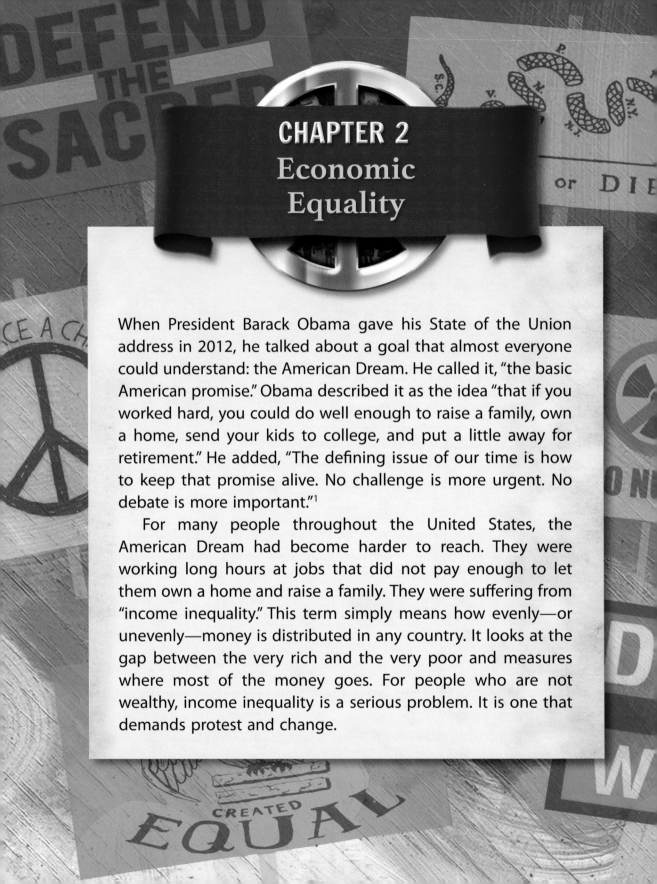

CHAPTER 2
Economic Equality

When President Barack Obama gave his State of the Union address in 2012, he talked about a goal that almost everyone could understand: the American Dream. He called it, "the basic American promise." Obama described it as the idea "that if you worked hard, you could do well enough to raise a family, own a home, send your kids to college, and put a little away for retirement." He added, "The defining issue of our time is how to keep that promise alive. No challenge is more urgent. No debate is more important."[1]

For many people throughout the United States, the American Dream had become harder to reach. They were working long hours at jobs that did not pay enough to let them own a home and raise a family. They were suffering from "income inequality." This term simply means how evenly—or unevenly—money is distributed in any country. It looks at the gap between the very rich and the very poor and measures where most of the money goes. For people who are not wealthy, income inequality is a serious problem. It is one that demands protest and change.

The first Occupy Wall Street event in 2011 focused on income inequality. The movement has inspired people to protest and has raised global awareness of other important issues.

Occupy protesters came in all colors and costumes. Some dressed in masks mirroring the freedom fighter from the film "V for Vendetta."

On Friday, September 16, 2011, Manhattan's Zuccotti Park was just another park in New York City. It was located near some of the country's largest banks and financial companies. A mere 24 hours later, according to the group's mission statement, it was home to a "leaderless resistance movement with people of many colors, genders and political persuasions."[2] The group came to be known as Occupy Wall Street, or the 99 Percenters. This nickname refers to the idea that one percent of the people in the United States own 99 percent of the money. The protesters represented the other 99 percent of the people.

One protester stated, "The one thing we all have in common is that we are the 99 percent that will no longer tolerate the greed and corruption of the one percent."[3] For the 99 percent, it is tough to make ends meet on

current wages. People are getting tired of the rich getting richer and the poor getting poorer.

The movement began with 1,000 protesters. Within weeks, the idea spread. Demonstrators showed up in more than 100 cities across the United States, and 1,500 cities around the world. Alec Courtney, a young man unemployed in New York, said, "The hope . . . is to show that through nonviolent protest, we can change this country. People can change. The government can change."[4]

Several celebrities took part in the protest, including actress Susan Sarandon and filmmaker Michael Moore. In early October, protesters dressed up as "corporate zombies." They wore suits and ties, and some were covered with fake money.[5]

A number of protesters used the pop culture fascination with zombies to show how large corporations are digesting people's brains and lives.

Occupy protests were held all around the world. In northern Hong Kong, main roads were completely blocked by as many as 100,000 people. When police used tear gas to move them, it only served to bring out more protesters.

While some people considered the protesters heroes, others were not impressed. At times demonstrators got out of hand. Police were forced to use pepper spray and make arrests. The protests lasted several months before people finally disbanded.

This grassroots organization helped people realize that the struggle to make ends meet was widespread. It also focused the nation on raising the minimum wage for workers throughout the country.

The 99 Percenters encouraged others to speak out also. In New York City, fast-food workers walked off their jobs to demand higher hourly wages. In April, thousands of workers marched across the U.S. to demand higher pay. Some companies, including Wal-Mart Stores and McDonalds, raised their hourly pay rates.[6]

The Occupy Movement has inspired a number of other protests. On April 13, 2016, for example, almost 40,000 workers stood up from their desks at Verizon and walked out. For 10 months they had worked to improve their wages, but their paychecks remained the same. They picketed. To show support for their cause, local businesses brought food and wrote encouraging letters to newspaper editors. Less than two months later, the workers all walked back in with much better contracts in place.[7]

Inspired by the Past

Although the Occupy Movement happened recently, it was partly motivated by protests of the past. During the country's Great Depression (1929–1939), money lost its value. The unemployment rate kept climbing. People stood in line for food. Banks foreclosed left and right, taking people's homes. Americans were terrified.

Neighbors protested the forced sale of a farmer's property during the Great Depression. They showed up for the auction, but then refused to bid.

Some farmers, in an attempt to profit from their produce, tried to keep some of their crops off the market. If they made their apples and corn harder to get, they thought, demand would go up and so would the prices. Protesters stepped in. They did not allow these farmers to reach the markets at all. Protesters in Iowa and Nebraska blocked roads. They poured milk onto the ground and turned cattle around to head back home.[8]

Not all farmers were in the same boat. In 1933, many of them were losing their land to foreclosure. Finally, thousands of angry farmers went to Lincoln, Nebraska, to march on the capitol building. They demanded the banks stop taking people's farms. The banks stopped foreclosing, but they allowed the local courts to decide for how long. It was not until President Franklin D. Roosevelt introduced new federal programs, often called The New Deal, that the country's economic depression began to fade. Farmers could finally get back to business.[9]

President Franklin Delano Roosevelt signed a number of acts as part of the New Deal. It helped turn the country in a stronger, healthier direction.

The Strike Heard Around the World

The men had had enough. They wanted better pay and safer working conditions. So, a day before a new year began, they decided to stop working, lock the doors, and . . . sit down. It was one of the country's first sit-down strikes, earning the nickname "the strike that was heard around the world."

On December 30, 1936, the autoworkers in the Detroit, Michigan General Motors plant went on strike. They locked themselves in the plant and let their demands be known. They wanted to join the United Auto Workers Union. The union would help workers to set up a fair minimum wage scale, put safety procedures in place, and provide a way for workers to express their concerns. General Motors refused.

For 44 days, the two sides battled. Inside the factory, the men played board games and waited. GM turned off the plant's heat, so the men put on coats and blankets to stay warm. When GM tried to stop the food supplies being brought to the strikers, a riot started. Strikers and police officers were hurt.

It did not take long for the strike's effect to ripple through GM. Production dropped from 50,000 cars in December to a mere 125 in February. Finally, GM admitted defeat. They signed an agreement with the union. The workers had won! More than that, they motivated other workers to follow their protest example. Within two weeks of their victory, more than 87 strikes began—in Detroit alone.[10]

Strikers guard the windows at the auto plant.

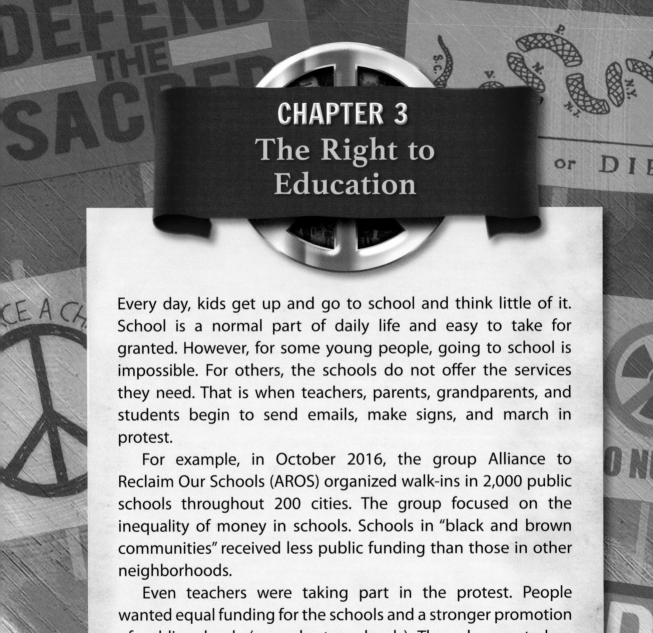

CHAPTER 3
The Right to Education

Every day, kids get up and go to school and think little of it. School is a normal part of daily life and easy to take for granted. However, for some young people, going to school is impossible. For others, the schools do not offer the services they need. That is when teachers, parents, grandparents, and students begin to send emails, make signs, and march in protest.

For example, in October 2016, the group Alliance to Reclaim Our Schools (AROS) organized walk-ins in 2,000 public schools throughout 200 cities. The group focused on the inequality of money in schools. Schools in "black and brown communities" received less public funding than those in other neighborhoods.

Even teachers were taking part in the protest. People wanted equal funding for the schools and a stronger promotion of public schools (over charter schools). They also wanted an end to harsh student discipline in the classrooms.

Keron Blair, director of AROS, told ThinkProgress, "Many schools in Black and Brown communities across the country

Many people participated in the 2016 AROS protest. They demanded better schools for their children and the young people in their communities.

Many young people spoke out for their schools, letting everyone know what they like—and what they want to change.

are called failing. But it is the students, parents and educators that have been failed."[1]

Erica Huerta, a teacher in East Los Angeles, believes that protests like this will bring important changes. "It's an exciting time, however bleak the situation looks," she stated. "The fact that there is a national alliance to reclaim our schools and that people are starting to talk about these issues across the state and across the country and maybe coordinating actions together—I think that's really exciting."[2]

Around the World

Laws are different in different countries. So are people's rights. In other countries, people rally for rights in education that may be taken for granted in the United States.

In 2016, students from the Royal College of the Blind protested outside Westminster.

In June 2016, almost two dozen students with special needs protested outside the Houses of Parliament in London, England. In the "Right, Not a Fight" campaign, the students demanded the same rights as mainstream students. They wanted the same guidance in college and career choices as all other students.

Joey Mander, a seventeen-year-old student, told *Coventry Observer* that he had attended a mainstream school. It was a hard experience. "I wasn't accepted and I couldn't get the support I needed," he said. "I was struggling to cope with the world because of my autism and didn't know where to get the help I needed."[3]

The protesters also wanted college options geared for the students' special needs. "There are places that we can learn at our own pace, where we get additional support and nobody says, 'Oh, you must be thick [stupid] then,'" said eighteen-year-old Dan Crossfield. " . . . specialist colleges are 'can do' places, where people don't put a ceiling on your aspirations, they say, 'Yes—go for it—give it a try.' "[4]

In some other countries, girls often have no chance of going to school. In Ethiopia, Guinea, and Niger, for example, fewer than 35 girls go to school for every 100 boys. In South and West Asia, approximately 87 girls start school for every 100 boys that attend.[5]

In some countries such as Pakistan and Afghanistan, hundreds of schools that accept female students have been closed, bombed, or burned down by religious groups. These groups believe that girls do not need an education. They teach instead that girls only need to become wives. In these places, girls are married, to older men, at age twelve or younger.

Girls are pushing back. In India, teenage girls are banding together to become "wedding busters." They create "child-marriage-free zones," promising each other they will stay in school and refuse to be married.

In Pakistan 2012, Kainat Riaz was shot on the way to school by the Taliban. This military group enforces extreme religious laws. Despite the danger, Riaz told the *New York Times* that she no longer hides her schoolbooks. She says the Taliban "can't stop us from going to school. I want to study. I am not afraid. We are strong."[6]

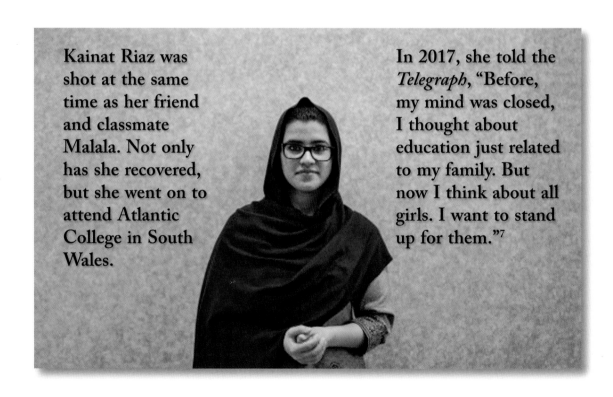

Kainat Riaz was shot at the same time as her friend and classmate Malala. Not only has she recovered, but she went on to attend Atlantic College in South Wales.

In 2017, she told the *Telegraph*, "Before, my mind was closed, I thought about education just related to my family. But now I think about all girls. I want to stand up for them."[7]

MALALA AND THE RIGHT TO BE EDUCATED

"I speak not for myself but for those without a voice . . . those who have fought for their rights . . . their right to live in peace, their right to be treated with dignity, their right to equality of opportunity, their right to be educated."

~ Malala Yousafzai, speaking before the United Nations, 2013[8]

On October 9, 2012, Malala Yousafzai was riding home in a school bus. On the way, she was shot in the head. The shot was meant to kill her. The gunmen were punishing the fifteen-year-old girl for speaking out against the Taliban, which denied many young women the chance for a good education.

Malala had given a number of speeches, titled "How Dare the Taliban Take Away My Basic Right to Education?" She was also featured in a *New York Times* documentary called *Class Dismiss*ed. She wrote an online blog for the English news channel BBC. (For that, she used the pen name Gul Makai.) For speaking out, she was awarded Pakistan's first national peace prize.[9]

The Taliban had planned to silence Malala forever. However, she survived the attack.

In March 2013, she returned to school in England. Since then, the young woman has dedicated her life to protesting the lack of quality education for women in many countries. Thanks to her courage and nonviolent protests, Malala helped inspire Pakistan to create its first Right to Education bill.[10]

Malala Yousafzai

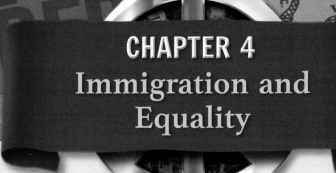

CHAPTER 4
Immigration and Equality

In November 2016, after the presidential election, women in the United States began talking about marching in January 2017. It did not take long for the word to spread.

On January 21, the world was shocked at just how many women came out to make a stand. Across the country, city streets filled with women (and men), most of them wearing pink hats with cat ears. Hundreds of thousands flooded Washington, D.C., marching to the White House. In cities such as New York, Chicago, Los Angeles, Boston, and Phoenix, thousands marched. Celebrities including Scarlett Johansson, America Ferrera, and Michael Moore made speeches. Marchers in other cities around the world joined them.

Although it is almost impossible to know how many people participated in the march, journalists estimate the number was between 3.5 and 4 million people. Some were there to stand up for women's rights, which they felt would be threatened by the newly elected president, Donald J. Trump. Some showed up with signs about climate change. Others carried signs about equal pay for equal jobs. Several women also spoke out against promised changes to the nation's immigration policies.[1]

The Women's March in 2017 drew more people and more media coverage than anyone expected. It also inspired people across the planet to stand up and speak out—with or without a pink hat.

At the turn of the twentieth century, immigrants still filled passenger steamships bound for the United States. For some, entrance would be impossible.

The United States has a long history of welcoming—and rejecting—immigrants. For the first century of America's history, thousands of immigrants came to the country from Ireland, Germany, and China. They brought their customs and beliefs. They competed for American jobs. This made many people angry. In response, in 1882, Congress put a limit on the number of Chinese immigrants it would allow into the country each year. That law stayed in place for more than 20 years.

Later, immigrants from Europe began arriving in the United States in large numbers. In 1917, Congress declared that all immigrants had to be able to read English to get into the country. The Immigration Act of 1924 limited the total number of foreigners who could move to the United States. It also established set numbers, or quotas, based on the immigrants' country of origin. Few from Eastern Europe and Africa were allowed. Those from most Asian countries were not allowed at all. This law was not revised until 1952.[2]

Other immigration bans have become part of U.S. history. In 1950, the McCarran Act banned anyone suspected of being a communist from coming into the country. In 1980, President Jimmy Carter banned anyone from Iran from entering the nation. In 1987, President Ronald Reagan banned anyone who was HIV positive from coming to the United States.[3]

Day Without Immigrants

In 2006, people across the United States spoke out against immigration limits. Many of them were protesting the Sensenbrenner bill. If it passed in the U.S. Senate, it would become a crime to provide food, housing, or medical help to illegal immigrants.

On March 1, downtown Chicago was packed with more than 100,000 protesters. Most of them were Latino. They chanted, *"Si, se puede,"* or "Yes, it

Young and old participated in the "Day without Immigrants" protest. They wanted people to know that the country was built on a long history of immigrants.

In Los Angeles, protesters raise a flag.

can be done."[4] In Los Angeles, 500,000 people gathered for the same reason. Denver, Houston, and San Diego had 75,000 protesters. In the end, 140 cities in 39 states took part in what became known as The Day Without Immigrants, or The Great American Boycott.[5] People blew whistles. They banged on drums. Signs read, "The U.S. Is Made by Immigrants!" In addition to protests, people boycotted shops and stayed home from work and school. Some protesters linked arms, creating long human chains. They waved banners that read, "We Die in the Desert for Beans."

The protesters wanted people to know how important immigrants were to the country's economy. As one protester stated, "We are the backbone of what America is, legal or illegal it doesn't matter. We butter each other's bread. They need us as much as we need them."[6]

In October 2015, immigrants found a different way to protest—by sending flowers. The Department of Homeland Security made a mistake on the department's website. Suddenly, as many as 150,000 immigrants were eligible to get their green cards. They were thrilled—until a few days later. That's when Homeland Security issued a bulletin saying they had made a mistake. One third of those applications were no longer valid. Those people would have to wait at least another ten years to become U.S. citizens.

The immigrants were upset. They responded by sending beautiful flowers to Jeh Johnson, Secretary of Homeland Security. They included cards that read, "Dear Honorable Jeh Johnson, DHS Visa Bulletin reversal has caused irreparable harm to our families. We ask you to not inflict injustice on us . . . for no fault of ours. Please fix the . . . bulletin. We wish you the very best."[7]

Immigration laws often tear families apart.

A New President and a New Ban

It's our right as a sovereign nation to choose immigrants that we think are the likeliest to thrive and flourish and love us.

—U.S. President Donald J. Trump[8]

In late January 2017, President Trump signed an executive order. It banned citizens from seven Muslim countries from entering the United States. Across the United States, thousands of demonstrators flooded airports in major cities. In San Francisco, protesters chanted, "You put up a wall, we tear it down!" Signs proclaimed, "One Earth, One People, One Love." In Boston, signs read, "No Human Is Illegal!" In Chicago, people chanted, "The whole world is watching!" In Los Angeles, the chant was, "Free them now!"[9]

Governors, mayors, and even senators joined the demonstrators. Massachusetts Senator Elizabeth Warren, a Democrat known for opposing many of President Trump's actions, joined the Boston protest. In New York, Governor Andrew Cuomo stated, "I never thought I'd see the day when refugees, who have fled war-torn countries in search of a better life, would be turned away at our doorstep. . . .This is not who we are, and not who we should be."[10] Senator Cory Booker of New Jersey was at Washington Dulles International Airport near Washington, D.C. "This will be an ongoing battle," he stated.[11]

At John F. Kennedy International Airport in New York, taxi drivers supported the protest. They went on strike until the ban was lifted. A federal judge in New York issued a stay that kept immigrants who were suddenly stranded in airports from being deported.

Thousands of people flooded JFK Airport in New York to protest President Trump's immigration ban.

Many of these protesters were fueled by moral outrage. Others knew the ban was basically illegal. More than 50 years before, Congress had outlawed this type of discrimination. The Immigration and Nationality Act was created in 1965, after the country had spent years barring immigrants from China and Japan.

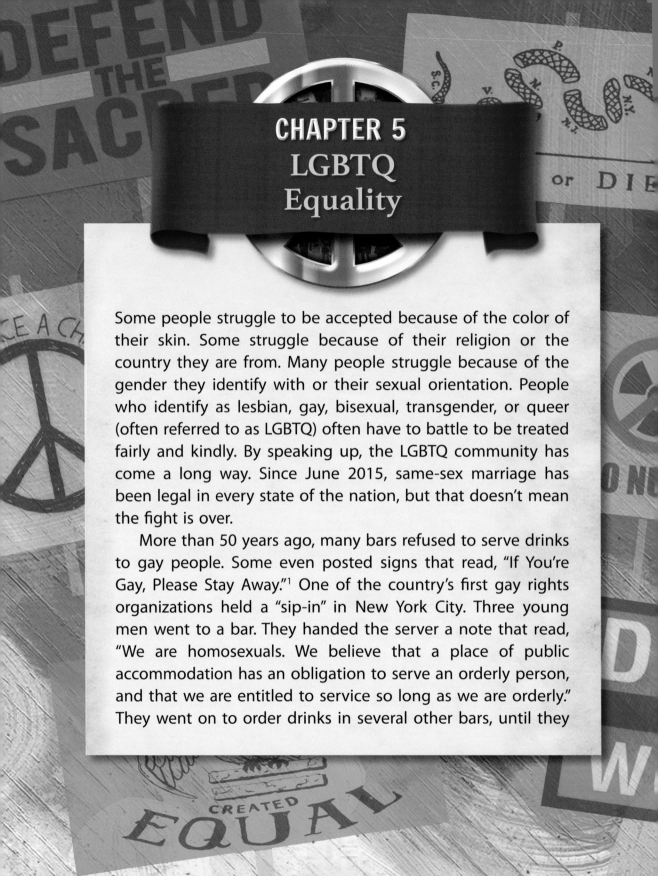

CHAPTER 5
LGBTQ
Equality

Some people struggle to be accepted because of the color of their skin. Some struggle because of their religion or the country they are from. Many people struggle because of the gender they identify with or their sexual orientation. People who identify as lesbian, gay, bisexual, transgender, or queer (often referred to as LGBTQ) often have to battle to be treated fairly and kindly. By speaking up, the LGBTQ community has come a long way. Since June 2015, same-sex marriage has been legal in every state of the nation, but that doesn't mean the fight is over.

More than 50 years ago, many bars refused to serve drinks to gay people. Some even posted signs that read, "If You're Gay, Please Stay Away."[1] One of the country's first gay rights organizations held a "sip-in" in New York City. Three young men went to a bar. They handed the server a note that read, "We are homosexuals. We believe that a place of public accommodation has an obligation to serve an orderly person, and that we are entitled to service so long as we are orderly." They went on to order drinks in several other bars, until they

Across the country, people are reaching out to LGBTQ people to let them know people care and stand behind them and their rights.

were finally refused. Two years later, the question of serving gays went to the Supreme Court. The judge ruled that gay people could not be refused service, stating, "their status does not make them criminals or outlaws."[2]

In the early morning hours of June 28, 1969, police raided a gay club in New York City called the Stonewall Inn. At that time, gay bars were routinely refused liquor licenses, because "acting gay" was declared to be "disorderly conduct." The police knew this club was serving alcohol, even though it did not have a liquor license.

The gay community was tired of seeing their bars shut down. People began yelling. Bottles were tossed at police officers. People marched in the streets. This riot has been called the first major protest for LGBTQ equal rights.

New York's Stonewall Inn is still open and a popular spot to visit. It bears a rainbow flag to show its support for the LGBTQ community.

People often gather in front of the Stonewall Inn to show their support of LGBTQ rights.

In 2016, the Stonewall Inn was named a national monument. President Obama stated, "The Stonewall Uprising is considered by many to be the catalyst that launched the modern LGBTQ civil rights movement. From this place and time, building on the work of many before, the nation started the march—not yet finished—toward securing equality and respect for LGBTQ people."[3]

In 2016, a lone gunman killed 49 gay people at the Pulse nightclub in Orlando, Florida. Thousands of LGBTQ New Yorkers flocked to the Stonewall Inn to leave flowers and cards. Many stayed to hold a vigil. Stacy Lentz, co-owner of the Stonewall Inn, told The *New York Times*, "The LGBTQ community has survived so much before, from AIDS to hate crimes. And we're continuing to show that we're strong and love wins."[4]

Across the street from the Stonewall Inn in Christopher Park is a set of bronze statues called *Gay Liberation*.

When a mall security officer removed a gay couple for holding hands at the Westfield Galleria in Roseville, California, the gay community was upset. They posted on Facebook that they wanted to sponsor a Love Is Love event. On March 9, 2013, approximately 250 LGBTQ couples came to the mall to kiss, hold hands, and dance. The mall's vice president of development addressed the crowd, stating, "It is time for a revolution. We cannot accept discrimination anymore."[5]

LGBTQ people have worked hard to earn equal rights in the United States. In other countries, however, the fight seems almost impossible. Homosexuality is considered a crime in countries such as India, Nigeria, and Russia. There, same-sex marriages and public displays of affection are illegal. In other countries, such as Iran, Saudi Arabia, Sudan, and Yemen, being gay is punishable by death.[6]

The ninth Bengaluru Pride Parade in India was held in 2016. In February 2017, the Indian Health Ministry began allowing schools to counsel teens that same-sex attraction is normal.

The Gay Liberation Day Parade in 1970 was the inspiration for the parades that continue today.

A Tradition of Pride

In 1970, one year after the riot at Stonewall Inn, activists celebrated by holding Christopher Street Gay Liberation Day. It came to be known as the country's first Gay Pride Parade. It was a radical idea at the time. "In those days, the idea of walking in daylight, with a sign saying, 'I'm a faggot,' was horrendous," said Doric Wilson in a documentary made about Stonewall. "Nobody, nobody was ready to do that." During that first parade, thousands of people marched through Manhattan, from Greenwich Village to Central Park. They chanted, "Say it clear, say it loud. Gay is good, gay is proud."[7]

Gay pride parades have been held every year since 1970 in cities throughout the world. At the 1978 San Francisco Pride Parade, the first rainbow flag was flown. Designed by Gilbert Baker, each color represents an important element: hot pink (sexuality), red (life), orange (healing), yellow (sunlight), green (nature), turquoise (magic), blue (harmony), and violet (spirit). Later, the hot pink and turquoise were dropped.

In Oslo, Norway, the EuroPride Parade focuses on honoring LGBTQ rights.

Today, pride parades feature floats, political speeches, and entertainers. In many places, the parade is only one part of a weeklong celebration called Pride Week. It includes dance parties, film festivals, and contests. In Europe, the parade is called EuroPride. Pride parades are held across the globe, including parts of Australia and Africa.

It often feels as if the world is too big for a single person to change it. However, as Holocaust survivor Elie Wiesel once said, "There may be times when we are powerless to prevent injustice, but there must never be a time when we fail to protest."[8] History is changed when people see inequality and unfairness and take the time to stand up, speak out, and say, "I protest!"

A Queer Dance Party

Some protesters march. Some sing. Some wave signs or banners. In January 2017, a group of people found a different way to send their message. They danced. Blasting the music of Beyoncé, Michael Jackson, and Madonna, about 200 members of the gay community headed out for Vice President Mike Pence's home in Washington, D.C. They walked over a mile to his neighborhood, dancing, singing, and handing out rainbow flags and glow sticks. Some protesters wore tutus and heels. Others donned gold party hats and light-up hula hoops. Pence, the former governor of Indiana, had frequently spoken out against same-sex marriage and LGBTQ rights.

The event was organized by the founder of WERK for Peace, a "queer-based grassroots movement that uses dance to promote peace."[9] Leader Firas Nasr told CNN, "We are here tonight to send a clear message to Daddy Pence that we will not tolerate bigotry and hate in our country." He added,

"Dance is a form of healing. It allows us to tap into our bodies and use our bodies, use movement to promote a movement."

Although the dancers could not reach Pence's house—and he was not even home at the time—they still made a statement. People living nearby came out to watch the parade, many of them cheering on the dancers.[10]

Sometimes the best way to make a point involves music and dancing.

It's Your Turn to Stand Up, Speak Out, and Protest

1. Make sure you have all of the facts and details about what you are protesting. You don't want to start a protest and then find it is all a misunderstanding.
2. Talk to your parents, teachers, or other trusted adults about your concerns. Ask if they can help you organize a protest.
3. Find other people who are also concerned about the issue. Ask them to participate in your protest.
4. Decide the best way to make your concerns known. It might be a speech at school, an article for the online newspaper, a picket outside a public place, or a local march. Talk to your school principal about it so that he or she understands what you have planned.
5. Announce the protest in school, as well as on social media sites such as Facebook, Twitter, and Instagram.
6. Reach out to local news reporters and invite them to come to the protest. If they do, they can help spread your message and get the public involved.
7. Know exactly what you want to achieve with your protest and focus on it.
8. Make signs to hold up at your event. Be sure that the signs have strong messages that are written clearly, and spelled and punctuated correctly.
9. At your protest, stay calm and polite. Getting angry, yelling, cursing, or getting violent is not only dangerous, but it damages your message.
10. Be ready to calmly, clearly, and politely explain to anyone who is curious why you are protesting and the reasons and facts behind your opinions.

Remember, protesting is your right! As politician Russ Feingold once said, "There is nothing more American than peaceful protest."

1868	The 14th Amendment grants all U.S. citizens "equal protection under the law."
1869	National Woman Suffrage Association is formed in New York City.
1882	Congress limits the number of Chinese people who can immigrate to the United States.
1908	The first suffrage parade is held.
1913	Thousands of women march for the right to vote. Woodrow Wilson is inaugurated.
1917	Suffragettes picket the White House. The U.S. Congress declares that immigrants will not be allowed to stay unless they can read and write English.
1920	The 19th Amendment gives women the right to vote.
1924	The Immigration Act limits how many people from each country may immigrate to the United States each year.
1929	The Great Depression begins.
1933	President Franklin D. Roosevelt begins enacting New Deal programs.
1936	Workers at General Motors stage a sit-down strike to improve wages and working conditions. Their protest convinces the automaker to sign a contract with United Auto Workers (UAW).
1950	The McCarran Act bans suspected communists from entering the country.
1969	Police raid the Stonewall Inn, a gay nightclub in New York City.
1970	Women gather in New York City for the Strike for Equality March.
1980	President Jimmy Carter bans anyone from Iran from entering the country.
2006	Marchers in 140 cities in 39 states protest the Sensenbrenner bill in The Great American Boycott.
2011	On June 17, women in Saudi Arabia protest for their rights by driving cars. On September 16, the Occupy Wall Street movement begins in Zuccotti Park, New York.
2013	About 250 gay couples protest for equality in the Love Is Love event at a mall in California.
2015	Citing the 14th Amendment, the U.S. Supreme Court declares same-sex marriage is legal in all fifty states. Women in Saudi Arabia win the right to vote.
2016	Workers at Verizon successfully strike for better contracts. Students with special needs rally in London, England, in the "Right Not a Fight" campaign. LGBTQ rallies protest the killing of 49 people in Orlando, Florida's Pulse nightclub. The Alliance to Reclaim Our Schools organizes walk-ins to address unequal funding in black and brown communities.
2017	On January 21, people around the world support U.S. marchers protesting impending threats to the rights of women and immigrants in the United States.

Chapter One

1. BrainyQuote. "Elizabeth Cady Stanton Quotes." https://www.brainyquote.com/quotes/quotes/e/elizabethc400013.html
2. Blakemore, Erin. "The Real Women's Suffrage Milestone That Just Turned 100." *Time*, October 23, 2015. http://time.com/4081629/suffrage-parade-1915/
3. The Library of Congress. "Tactics and Techniques of the National Woman's Party Suffrage Campaign." *American Memory*. Undated. https://www.loc.gov/collections/static/women-of-protest/images/tactics.pdf
4. Inez Haynes Irwin, *The Story of Alice Paul and the National Woman's Party* (Fairfax, VA: Denlinger's Publishers, 1920; reprint 1977). https://www.loc.gov/collections/static/women-of-protest/images/tactics.pdf
5. Amjoon, Mohammed. "Saudi Women Defy Driving Ban." *CNN*. June 20, 2011. http://www.cnn.com/2011/WORLD/meast/06/17/saudi.women.drivers/
6. Ibid.
7. Cohen, Sasha. "The Day Women Went on Strike." *Time*, August 26, 2015. http://time.com/4008060/women-strike-equality-1970/
8. Dylan, Bob. "Blowin' in the Wind." http://www.azlyrics.com/lyrics/bobdylan/blowininthewind.html
9. Greene, Andy. "Readers' Poll: The 10 Best Protest Songs of All Time." *Rolling Stone*. December 3, 2014. http://www.rollingstone.com/music/lists/readers-poll-the-10-best-protest-songs-of-all-time-20141203

Chapter Two

1. Harcourt, Bernard E. "Occupy Wall Street's 'Political Disobedience.'" *The New York Times*. October 13, 2011. https://opinionator.blogs.nytimes.com/2011/10/13/occupy-wall-streets-political-disobedience/?_r=0
2. Sutter, John. "What Is Income Inequality, Anyway?" *CNN.com*, October 29, 2013. http://www.cnn.com/2013/10/29/opinion/sutter-explainer-income-inequality/
3. "Occupy Wall Street: Fast Facts." *Guest of a Guest*. Undated. http://guestofaguest.com/new-york/instant-expert/occupy-wall-street
4. "Wall Street Demonstrators Dressed as 'Corporate Zombies' Lurch Past Stock Exchange as Protests Spread beyond America." *The Daily Mail*. October 4, 2011. http://www.dailymail.co.uk/news/article-2044983/Occupy-Wall-Street-protesters-dressed-corporate-zombies-lurch-past-stock-exchange-protests-spread-America.html
5. "Occupy Wall Street: A Protest Timeline." *The Week*, November 21, 2011. http://theweek.com/articles/481160/occupy-wall-street-protest-timeline
6. Levitin, Michael. "The Triumph of Occupy Wall Street." *The Atlantic*. June 10, 2015. http://www.theatlantic.com/politics/archive/2015/06/the-triumph-of-occupy-wall-street/395408/
7. Shelton, Chris. "A Strike for All Working Families." *Huffington Post*. June 17, 2016. http://www.huffingtonpost.comchris-shelton/a-strike-for-all-working_b_10533384.html
8. Ganzel, Bill. "Radical Farm Protests." *Farming in the 1930s*. 2003. http://www.livinghistoryfarm.org/farminginthe30s/money_11.html
9. Ibid.
10. This Day in History: "Sit-Down Strike Begins in Flint." *History.com*, 2010. http://www.history.com/this-day-in-history/sit-down-strike-begins-in-flint

Chapter Three

1. Clawson, Laura. "Teachers and Parents in 200 Cities Stage Walk-Ins for School Funding." *Daily Kos*. October 6, 2016. http://www.dailykos.com/story/2016/10/06/1578609/-Teachers-and-parents-in-200-cities-walk-in-for-school-funding
2. Quinlan, Casey. "Teachers in Over 200 Cities Protest Public School Funding." *Think Progress*, October 6, 2014. https://thinkprogress.org/teachers-in-over-200-cities-protest-public-school-funding-ffb1a8572025#.odj0o7igm
3. "Disabled Youngsters Protest against Educational Inequality." *Coventry Observer*, October 28, 2016. https://coventryobserver.co.uk/news/disabled-youngsters-protest-educational-inequality/
4. Ibid.
5. Chen, Michelle. "Why Girls Around the World Don't Get to Go to School." *Alternet,* September 23, 2010. http://www.alternet.org/story/148292 why_girls_around_the_world_don't_get_to_go_to_school
6. Brown, Gordon. "Girls Who Risk Their Lives for Education." *The New York Times*. April 8, 2013. http://www.nytimes.com/2013/04/09/opinion/global/gtirls-who-risk-their-lives-for-education.html
7. Smallman, Etan. "Meet the 'Other Malalas'—the Nobel Peace Prize Winner's Friends Now Heading to Edinburgh University." *The Telegraph*, April 18, 2017. http://www.telegraph.co.uk/women/life/meet-malalas-nobel-peace-prize-winners-friends-now-heading/

8. "Malala Tells UN: I Speak 'For Those Without a Voice.' " *NBC News*, July 12, 2013. http://www.nbcnews.com/video/nbc-news/52459793

9. Beck, Koa. "10 Fast Facts on Malala Yousafzai, the World's Youngest Nobel Peace Prize Winner." *Dailyworth*, October 10, 2014. https://www.dailyworth.com/posts/3014-10-fast-facts-about-malala-yousafzai

10 CNN Library. "Malala Yousafzai Fast Facts." *CNN.com*. June 23, 2016. http://www.cnn.com/2015/08/20/world/malala-yousafzai-fast-facts/

Chapter Four

1. Garber, Megan. "The Inauguration, and the Counter-Inauguration." *The Atlantic*. January 21, 2017. https://www.theatlantic.com/entertainment/archive/2017/01/the-inauguration-and-the-counter-inauguration/514055/

2. Office of the Historian, "The Immigration Act of 1924 (The Johnson-Reed Act)." *Department of State*. Undated. https://history.state.gov/milestones/1921-1936/immigration-act

3. "Six Other Times the U.S. Has Banned Immigrants." *Al Jazeera News*. January 29, 2017. http://www.aljazeera.com/indepth/features/2017/01/times-banned-immigrants-170128183528941.html

4. Engler, Mark, and Paul Engler. "The Massive Immigrant-Rights Protests of 2006 Are Still Changing Politics." *LA Times*. March 4, 2016. http://www.latimes.com/opinion/op-ed/la-oe-0306-engler-immigration-protests-2006-20160306-story.html

5. Glaister, Dan. "U.S. Counts Cost of Day without Immigrants." *The Guardian*. May 1, 2006. https://www.theguardian.com/world/2006/may/02/usa.topstories3

6. McKinley, Carol, et al. " 'A Day Without Immigrants.' " *Fox News*. May 1, 2006. http://www.foxnews.com/story/2006/05/01/day-without-immigrants.html

7. O'Brien, Sara Ashley. "Immigrants Protest with Flowers after Green Card Mixup." *CNN Money*. October 5, 2015. http://money.cnn.com/2015/10/05/news/economy/green-card-mixup/

8. Jones, Susan. "Trump: 'It Is Our Right . . . to Choose Immigrants' Who Are Likely to Flourish Here." *CNS News*. September 1, 2016. http://www.cnsnews.com/news/article/susan-jones/trump-it-our-right-to-choose-immigrants-who-are-likely-flourish-here

9. Bier, David. "Trump's Immigration Ban Illegal." *The New York Times. January 27, 2017. https://www.nytimes.com/2017/01/27/opinion/trumps-immigration-ban-is-illegal.html?_r=0*

10. Ibid.

11. Doubek, James. "Thousands Protest at Airports Nationwide against Trump's Immigration Order." *NPR: Oregon Public Broadcasting*. January 29, 2017. http://www.npr.org/sections/thetwo-way/2017/01/29/512250469/photos-thousands-protest-at-airports-nationwide-against-trumps-immigration-order

Chapter Five

1. Farber, Jim. "Before the Stonewall Uprising, There Was the 'Sip-In.'" *The New York Times*. April 20, 2016. https://www.nytimes.com/2016/04/21/nyregion/before-the-stonewall-riots-there-was-the-sip-in.html

2. Ibid.

3. Rosenburg, Eli. "Stonewall Inn Named National Monument, a First for the Gay Rights Movement." *The New York Times*. June 24, 2016. https://www.nytimes.com/2016/06/25/nyregion/stonewall-inn-named-national-monument-a-first-for-gay-rights-movement.html?rref=collection%2Ftimestopic%2FStonewall%20Rebellion

4. Remnick, Noah. "A Moment of Solidarity at the Stonewall Inn, a Gay Rights Landmark." *The New York Times*. June 13, 2016. https://www.nytimes.com/2016/06/14/nyregion/a-moment-of-solidarity-at-the-stonewall-inn-a-gay-rights-landmark.html?rref=collection%2Ftimestopic%2FStonewall%20Rebellion

5. Eifertsen, Robyn. "Showing Their Love: LGBT Couples Claim Equality at Roseville Mall." *Roseville Patch*. March 10, 2013. http://patch.com/california/roseville-ca/showing-their-love-lgbt-supporters#photo-13613861

6. BBC, "Where Is It Illegal to Be Gay?" *BBC News*. February 10, 2014. http://www.bbc.com/news/world-25927595

7. Wythe, Bianca. "How the Pride Parade Became Tradition." PBS.org. June 9, 2011. http://www.pbs.org/wgbh/americanexperience/blog/2011/06/09/pride-parade/

8. Wiesel, Elie. "Hope, Despair and Memory." *Nobel Prize.org*. December 11, 1986. http://www.nobelprize.org/nobel_prizes/peace/laureates/1986/wiesel-lecture.html

9. Zorthia, Julia. "LGBT Activists Had a Dance Party Protest in Mike Pence's Neighborhood." *Time*. January 19, 2017. http://time.com/4639152/mike-pence-queer-dance-party/

10. Reynolds, Megan. "Pro-LGBTQ Protesters Threw a 'Queer Dance Party' in Front of Mike Pence's House." *Jezebel*. January 18, 2017. http://jezebel.com/pro-lgbtq-protesters-threw-a-queer-dance-party-in-front-1791362019

Books

Bausum, Ann. *Stonewall: Breaking Out in the Fight for Gay Rights*. New York: Speak, Reprint Edition, 2016.

Corey, Shana. *Malala: A Hero for All*. New York: Random House Books for Young Readers, 2016.

Freedman, Russell. *Because They Marched: The People's Campaign for Voting Rights That Changed America*. New York: Holiday House, 2016.

Freedman, Russell. *We Will Not Be Silent: The White Rose Student Resistance Movement That Defied Adolf Hitler*. New York: Clarion Books, 2016.

Klein, Carol Swartout. *Painting for Peace in Ferguson*. St. Paul, MN: Treehouse Publishing Group, 2015.

Langston-George, Rebecca. *For the Right to Learn: Malala Yousafzai's Story*. Minneapolis, MN: Capstone Press, 2016.

Levy, Debbie. *I Dissent: Ruth Bader Ginsburg Makes Her Mark*. New York: Simon & Schuster Books for Young Readers, 2016.

Pinkney, Andrea Davis. *Sit In: How Four Friends Stood Up by Sitting Down*. Boston: Little, Brown Books for Young Readers, 2010.

Wilson, Janet. *Our Rights: How Kids Are Changing the World*. Toronto, ON: Second Story Press, 2013.

On the Internet

ACLU for Women's Rights
https://www.aclu.org/issues/womens-rights

Human Rights Campain
http://www.hrc.org/

Informed Immigrant
www.informedimmigrant.com/

alliance (uh-LY-untz)—A group of people or organizations that have agreed to work together for a common purpose.

amendment (ah-MEND-ment)—A change to a legal document, such as to the Constitution of the United States.

autism (AW-tism)—A developmental disorder that makes it hard for a person to interact and communicate with other people.

boycott (BOY-kot)—To refuse to buy goods or attend an event in order to make a statement.

catalyst (KAT-uh-list)—Something that causes or speeds up a significant change in something else.

deport (dee-PORT)—To expel or force a foreigner to leave a country.

foreclose (for-CLOHZ)—To take away a person's property for lack of payment.

grassroots (gras-REWTS)—Fundamental; involving the common people as an important political group.

green card—A permit issued by the U.S. government that allows a non-citizen to live and work permanently in the United States.

inauguration (in-awg-yur-AY-shun)—The ceremony that officially gives a person a new political position.

irreparable (ee-REP-ruh-bul)—Beyond repair.

mainstream (MAYN-streem)—Considered normal, ordinary, or common.

petition (peh-TIH-shun)—An official request or demand signed by many people.

quota (KWOH-tuh)—A fixed number or share.

racism (RAY-sih-sm)—The belief that a person's race determines his or her traits.

rally (RAL-ee)—To gather for a cause.

resign (ree-ZYN)—To quit a job.

suffrage (SUH-fridj)—The right to vote.

suffragette (suf-ruh-JET)—A woman who fights for the right to vote.

Taliban (TAH-lih-ban)—A militant group that enforces strict religious laws without regard to civil laws.

transitory (TRANS-ih-tor-ee)—Passing quickly; not permanent or lasting.

vigil (VIH-jul)—A period of watchfulness, support, and prayer, usually at night.